You
Make
the World
Better

We live in a world filled with wonderful things—
with city lights and favorite places, with fantastic
opportunities, grand surprises, and plenty of special
moments in between. But these aren't the only things
that make our world a delight. And they aren't the
only things that make life rich. Because what really
brings these wondrous things to life are the people
we know—the ones who make the adventure worth
taking, the ones who turn experiences into memories,
the ones who make the world better.

You're one of those people. You add joy, humor, and meaning. You turn regular days into a celebration. And you can always be counted on to do something, no matter how simple it may seem, that will add extra to the ordinary.

Thanks for being you. Thanks for all the things you do. *You make the world better.*

Those who bring sunshine
to the lives of others cannot
keep it from themselves.

J.M. Barrie

You are a
LIGHT.

...we make a life by
what we give.

Winston Churchill

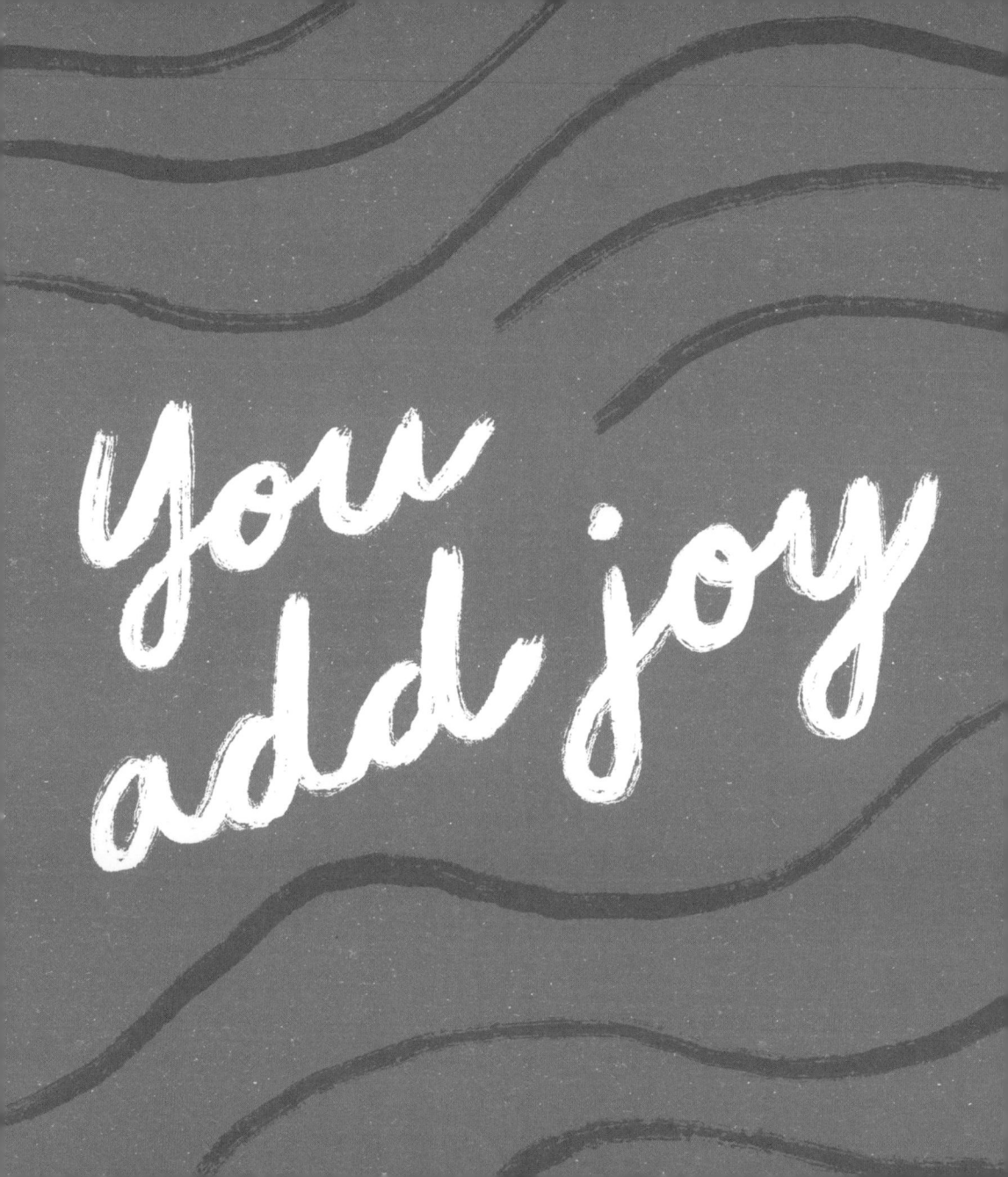

to every day.

Go out into the world
and do good until there is too
much good in the world.

Larry H. Miller

YOU MAKE LIFE
sweeter.

Blessed are those who can give without remembering and take without forgetting.

Elizabeth Bibesco

You are an
inspiration.

By being yourself, you put something wonderful in the world that was not there before.

Edwin Elliot

You
add extra

to the
ordinary.

Ah, life grows lovely
where you are...

Mathilde Blind

YOU MAKE
EACH DAY MORE
beautiful.

Your thoughts, words
and deeds are painting
the world around you.

Jewel Diamond Taylor

You are a
MARVEL.

Every sunrise is an
invitation for us to arise and
brighten someone's day.

Richelle E. Goodrich

You add
heart
to all
you do.

What a difference one person can make!

Sasha Azevedo

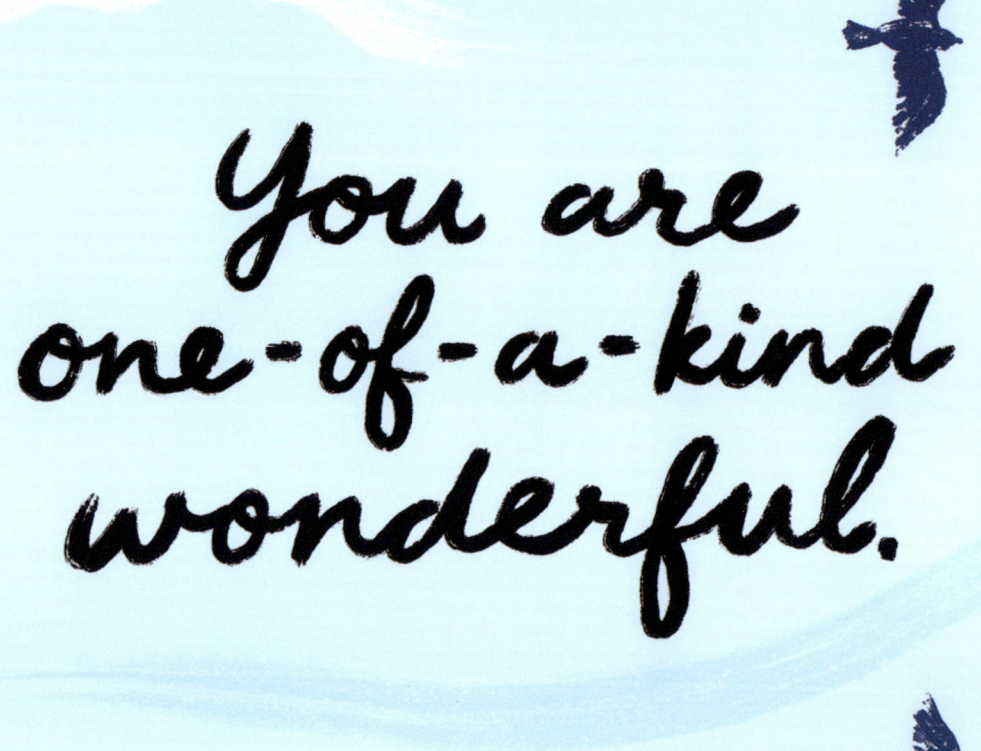

You are
one-of-a-kind
wonderful.

Act your heart.
There's nothing else.

Theodore Roethke

YOU ALWAYS
add joy.

May happiness touch your
life today as warmly as you have
touched the lives of others.

Rebecca Forsythe

You
bring out

the best
in people.

Some people look for
a beautiful place. Others
make a place beautiful.

Inayat Khan

YOU CHANGE
THINGS
for the
better.

Fill each day with
light and heart.

John Tillotson

You create a
brighter
world.

COMPENDIUM.
live inspired

An imprint of the Crown Publishing Group
A division of Penguin Random House LLC
1745 Broadway, New York, NY 10019
live-inspired.com | penguinrandomhouse.com

Library of Congress Control Number: 2023943008 | ISBN: 978-1-957891-33-0

Writer: Jennifer Pletsch and M.H. Clark
Designer: Jessica Phoenix
Editor: Miriam Hathaway
Production Manager: Shannon Lery

2nd printing. Manufactured in China with soy inks on FSC®-Mix certified paper.

The authorized representative in the EU for product safety and compliance is Penguin Random House
Ireland, Morrison Chambers, 32 Nassau Street, Dublin D02 YH68, Ireland, https://eu-contact.penguin.ie.

Create
meaningful
moments
with gifts
that inspire.

CONNECT WITH US
live-inspired.com | sayhello@compendiuminc.com

   @compendiumliveinspired
#compendiumliveinspired